THE TURN OF THE

For Sonia,

Wishing you a Merry
Christmas and Happy
New Year. 1998.

I thought the poems
are rather good
and Me Thinks! you
will enjoy!

David.

by the same author

*

Faint Heart Never Kissed a Pig (Routledge & Kegan Paul, 1982)
Sows' Ears and Silk Purses (Routledge & Kegan Paul, 1984)
Pearls Before Swine (Routledge & Kegan Paul, 1985)

The Turn of the Cucumber

ANN DRYSDALE

PETERLOO POETS

First published in 1995
by Peterloo Poets
2 Kelly Gardens, Calstock, Cornwall PL18 9SA, U.K.

A catalogue record for this book is available
from the British Library

ISBN 1-871471-48-6

Printed in Great Britain by
Latimer Trend & Company Ltd, Plymouth

ACKNOWLEDGEMENTS: 'Manifold Manor' first appeared in the *South Wales Argus*. 'Slugs, Mating' won 5th prize in the 1994 Peterloo Poets Open Poetry Competition and was published in the Peterloo Competition poster/leaflet of the same year.

For the ghosts between the pages
in lieu of flowers.

Contents

Page

THE SEVEN AGES OF THE SHE-POET

FROM FURTHER AFIELD

CODA

INTROIT:

The Turn of the Cucumber

For a long time I thought she was made-up.
Praxilla of Sicyon: poetess
Five hundred years before the birth of Christ.
Nobody else seemed to have heard of her.
Even my classical concordance
Jumps from Pratinas to Praxiteles.
She was a legend in her lifetime, though;
Tripped off the tongue of Grecian literati
In an amusing piece of Attic jargon —
"Sillier than Praxilla's Adonis".

This was because she cast Adonis' death
In something other than the classic mould.
Her hero dies regretting what he lost;
He mourns the sun and moon — so far so good —
But then extends his terminal regret
To cover smaller things. Apples. And pears.
And — inspired masterstroke — ripe cucumbers.

Thus was Praxilla laughed into oblivion
By pissed-off purists. Now we understand
The relative importance of such things;
We have reorchestrated the criteria;
We have developed a respect for trivia.

So now it is my turn; mine and Praxilla's.
At last it is the turn of the cucumber.

ARISINGS

" ... pieces of material left over from a job which are of value. They are collected
and may be sold, melted or made up again."
Admiralty Manual of Seamanship

Tin Wheels

They were the very first of my found things.
Two little wheels, joined by a metal rod,
Part of a cheap tin toy; all small enough
To huddle hidden in a toddler's hand.
I loved them dearly for their jolly roundness
Giggling along the flags at a finger-push.
I loved the having and the keeping-safe
Of this, the first fruit of my own finding.

An adult found the rust and the sharp edges.

I still recall the day I found them gone
And what was said. Even now, in lost nights
When I have "nothing better to cry for"
I wail as I did then:
"Gran says you threw my little wheels away".

They were the last love that I never hid;
They were my first irrevocable loss.

Aunt

Will I ever again think two consecutive thoughts?
The old quiet spaces are now full of you;
Strident in scarlet boots — Caligula!

You trudge on small, slow legs,
Waterfilled wellingtons sucking and plopping
At each exaggerated step.

You thwart attempts at speed:
Hold my hand? Don't then. I will go without you.
Alone. To run a bath. To put the kettle on.

The thought is unimaginably sweet. But guilt
Puts a constraining bracelet round my knees.
"Wait for me!" Yes, I will,
For if I don't, you'll tell
And I will lose face, jeopardise my status:
Auntie. Benign. Ever Benevolent.

But God forgive
The urge to pick the precious burden up
And run with it.

Cot Death

The funeral was too soon.
We knew that he had died
But had not come to where we could believe
That he was not alive; not here any more.

The service was too short.
I could still feel him —
The sweet, warm weight of him before they took him,
And left the emptiness, the nothing-weight.

The coffin was too big.
He would be lost in it.
It seemed unfair to leave him alone in it,
Leave him believing that we didn't know.

The flowers were too cruel.
Tastefully tiny posies.
All buds; no blossoms. All spewing gypsophila,
Known to those in the trade as "baby's breath".

Dear Jane ...

I got your letter, love; it came today.
I read it through and the knife went straight home.
No blood came to distract or fascinate,
No tears to give a focus to the pain;
Only the sad sameness of what was left.
A tumbled bed. One bar of the fire glowing.
An orphan piglet in a cardboard box.
I picked it up; it squealed on my behalf,
Pricked by the envelope still in my hand.
I saw us in the mirror, and our backs
Reflected in another glass behind —
Reflected back-to-back and back again.
So there we were: a woman with a pig,
Facing both ways at once, like January.
A torn-out cliché from a third-rate book:
"Frozen for ever into the fabric of time;
Travelling at the speed of light into infinity".

Two-Finger Exercises

one from the head; one from the heart

THE SCISSORS

Twenty disciples in a dusty gym,
All mirroring the master's martial arts.
Some half a dozen of them neat and trim
And all the rest with less-than-perfect parts.
There is no great compulsion to achieve,
No formal judgement of each person's skill
And yet one cannot help but half-believe
That all one's destiny for good or ill
Will be determined finally by how
One's pattern-cutter's scissored-up the bits.
I feel I should draw nearer to the Tao
If I had had a waist and proper tits.
How can one concentrate on formal form
While plainly flouting an informal norm?

(The Scissors is an especially ungainly posture adopted during the performance of the T'ai Chi form)

SLEI'S HAIKU

Cerebral sight-hound
Hand-knitted in hairy string,
His balls in tandem.

Slugs, Mating

Sixty-nine is the number of the beasts; they mate
Head-to-tail. Underfoot. Everywhere. Always.
I have seen them slipping alongside one another like slick ships
Passing (but never overtaking) in the night, wondering why
For years, because it was almost too simple to grasp.
Slugs are hermaphrodite;
Their basic little cunt-and-prick arrangement
Is in the same place on each and every slug.
No element of choice; sunwise or widdershins.
Each one both Cinderella and Prince Charming
With happy-ever-after guaranteed.
If they obey the rule of confrontation
The slipper always fits.
Such liberation! No more searching for equal and opposite.
No more jostling at parties
Like rooting in a box of nuts and bolts. Some of us
Would never again find ourselves cross-threaded,
Wrongfooted by a doublebreasted coat
And always dancing backwards.

Amanuensis

When we made love a hundred years ago
I obviously didn't do it right.
You chose not to repeat the exercise,
Even suggesting it might do me good
To sublimate my sexuality.
And so I did.

Now I massage your prose; slyly administer
A tongue-tip touch to your participles
So light that you should never know of it
And merely marvel at the consequence —
Relaxing into laughter and relief
Despite yourself.

I touched-up to the limit of my skill.
"I don't like that" you said; "it isn't me,"
"There's something wrong; show me the manuscript."
And with the clarity of *déja vu*,
I knew you knew.

Anita's Visit

"And are there many rooms upstairs?" she said,
Glancing about, her studied innocence
Asking the question: "Do you sleep together?"
I felt the urge to say "We share a bed
And sometimes, in the darkness, share each other —
A double question of convenience
And of communication. Hands convey
Hurting and healing, and our coupling, too,
Is sharing, showing things we would not say —
Inchoate, wishing-things that have to do
With care and comfort — and the tenderness
That follows leads to sleep. And letting-go.
Lovers asleep are no-one's but their own.
Together? No, my dear; we sleep alone."

Snoring

Snoring is such a churlish thing to do.
I can't imagine what I did it for,
Especially when I longed to sleep with you.

Given the choice, I'd rather fart than snore.
Snoring is an unlovely thing to do;
It makes me unacceptable to you.

You rose and sighed and strode and slammed the door.
You said it "didn't matter", but I knew
I couldn't leave you fuming on the floor.

"Leave me alone" you said. So I forbore
To argue, though I longed to call you through
And beg another chance to sleep with you.

Another chance. To sleep — perchance to snore —
Something I couldn't promise not to do;
So I crept sadly out through the back door.

Bereft, I left, and bade our bed adieu.
I'd gladly give an arm to know for sure
That I could sleep somewhere without a snore;
The other — and both legs — to sleep with you.

Queen of Puddings

for Mavis Carter

It's a long time since someone said to me
The things you said in *Pud* — your secret language,
Asking to be unravelled, like thieves' cant.

At first it was simply a taste of something.
A warm, strong taste, a bit like cinnamon.
Sweet but not sticky; simple but not plain.

Deeper than cosy childhood chocolate comfort.
Subtler than the seduction of whipped cream.
More than the giggle of a drop of booze.

And then I guessed. There was a word in it,
Like something silver in a Christmas pudding;
Something that you had hidden in its making.

I read the message in the Sherry Log.
I used some of that love to season this —
Can you taste it?

Persona Non Grata

One is aware of an enormous elbow
Far greater than the sum of its real parts.

You lead with it when you enter a room
With me in it. You make no eye contact
But execute a complicated dance
On the balls of your feet, tittuping;
A waggle-dance, telling your fellow B's
There is no sweetness here.

                    Slick choreography
But contrary to what you may suppose
It is not an exclusive manoeuvre.
I could make roomfuls of people do it
In perfect synchrony ... *"Yeeeeeeee-HAAR!*
    Sashay left and do-si-do
    Out with the elbow and OFF WE GO!"

They say you do it to make me feel small
But on the contrary I feel enormous
When you glide by on a diagonal,
Fastidiously circumnavigate
The unsavoury something in your path,
Holding the elbow in advance of you —
A steel boss on an invisible shield.

I feel called to impale myself on it
Like a failed Roman soldier on his sword.
Over-reaction? Probably. And yet —
Exquisite paradox — how is it possible
To bruise oneself on an imaginary elbow?

Through the Square Window

The sun slides through the glass on golden rods
Philip's small head, square on square shoulders, nods
And rises as he works. The square screen glows.
Old, ugly vinyl tiles lead in straight rows
To the long level desk; the straightbacked chair
Placed centrally — a square within a square,
And files and papers lie at random there —
A gathering of corners in his square
Domain. Anglepoise, awkward, stiff and still;
An upthrust elbow on the windowsill.
Behind his back, where only I can see
Three things challenge his fearful symmetry.
My jacket on the floor, a shapeless heap,
And, in a sunshine pool, two dogs, asleep.
Melding together in a dusty blur;
Amorphous, deliquescent piles of fur.

Total Quality Management

St. Ignatius speaks through a window in the schedule of Christ:

To labour and to ask for no reward
Save that of knowing that we do thy will —
I like to call it "God as Customer" —
Only a broad brush thing as yet, JC;
I had in mind to run it past the lads,
See if they pick it up and march with it.

A New Manager interprets the teachings of Ishikawa-san:

He wants two million bog-standard widgets
Turned out between now and next May
To a tolerant tolerance stated
As thousands of thou either way.

But can we just make him his widgets?
To freely agree to conform
To slovenly specification
Could tempt us to underperform.

So — all out for Excellence, people!
It's just not enough to do well;
We'll exceed his limpwristed requirements
Till we make him feel guilty as hell.

Mrs Prothero challenges the principles of W. Edwards Deming:

"A willing worker in a random process
May now and then achieve ten out of ten
When scooping red beads, say, from among white.
But to reward him for this happy fluke
Is pointless. Next time he may score a duck —
Must we condemn him then for laxity?"

Ah, but see yonder Mrs Prothero
Go tentatively to the Pick 'n' Mix.
See her approach the liquorice allsorts
To scoop a quarter for her little boy.
He loves the fat, square fondants; hates the ones
That look like belly-buttons full of warts.
See now the grocer watching from the door.
See Mrs Prothero avoid his stare,
Pick up the scoop and plunge it in the sweets.
Her face a mask of studied unconcern,
She carries back her booty to the scales.
Never in more than thirty of these trips
Have any belly-buttons got that far.
Is it a special flick of a skilled wrist?
A little linger where the fondants are?
It's what they call 'discretionary effort'
But I prefer to think of it as love.

Of Courses

I went on a course — well, I thought it was a course —
We worked very hard and achieved quite a lot;
But it didn't have a Theme Task or a Broad Brush Assessment,
So I had to conclude that it was not.

I went on a course that was more like a course —
The teachers didn't teach, they were Programmed to Direct
And Encourage Contribution to the Input on Concepts,
But it wasn't what I'd come to expect.

I went on a course — and it really was a course,
With Flip-charts and Modules and Running-with-the-Ball,
But nobody listened to it, nobody learned from it.
So it wasn't worth a shit, after all.

POETS' CORNER

Automatic Writing

Peach and parabola,
Weasel, muffet and fling.

Plush softness, soaring curve,
Sly, slinking shadow, soft fur-thing
And whizzing breathless flight.

Mysterious bubbles in a stream of consciousness or
Names in haste for a sudden panic of kittens or
Only words.

Words like only.

Lines to accompany a donation to the Poetry Society

Confucius say ...

A poor man in possession of two pence
Should spend one on a loaf, one on a flower.
This, on the face of it, is common sense.
But any hungry peasant in his hour
Of greatest need would rather overlook
His desperate, demeaning need to eat
And spend his tuppence on a little treat
Like forty Woodbines or a dirty book.
And thus this verse I venture to submit
To maximise the worth of my donation.
I know what starving souls should do with it;
I know the honest pauper's inclination —
So, notwithstanding what Kung Fu Tse said,
Buy two chrysanthemums. Bugger the bread.

Song of Innocence

We met again in Blackwell's, Blake and I —
A man whose simple songs I learned by rote
When I was ten years old and four foot high
And not empowered to detect the note
Of any genius that might be found
In battered babes, limp lambs and tygers taut,
All set about with craftsmanship unsound
And suspect syntax. Now I found my thought
Was not "How near to the obscure Divine
Comes, now and then, the questing soul of Man".
Rather "How faint is the dividing-line
Between the mystic and the charlatan".

And if it rains, a closed car at four

If the sun shines, we'll do it on the heath
Behind the bandstand on the flattened grass.
I'll wear the mink with nothing underneath;
You'll slide your jacket underneath my arse.
God! how I love a man in uniform!
We'll play the Countess and the Brigadier
And I'll chastise you if you can't perform
And you can plead for mercy in my ear.
At any moment we could be discovered.
That thought were aphrodisiac enough
Without the added frisson of a lover
As well-endowed as you, my bit of rough.

But if it rains, we'll have to take the Rover
And park it round behind the Little Chef.
By four the lunchtime rush should all be over;
And we'll occlude the windows with our breath.
We're neither of us getting any younger
And it's becoming something of a squeeze
To make with you, my back-seat muffin-monger,
The beast with two backs and a hundred knees.

Whichever way things fall out with the weather,
If sunshine blesses us or rain betrays,
We'll spend our regulation hour together
And then get dressed and go our separate ways.
We'll giggle and we'll beg each other's pardon,
Then I shall drive us back to Muswell Hill
Where you'll retrieve your pushbike from the garden
And whistle as you pedal home to Lil.

Winter Song

When blizzards blow under the tiles
And the dishcloth crisps on the draining-board
And the snowscape stretches for miles and miles
And only the idiot ventures abroad.
When it's early to bed, and thank heavens for that,
Then coldly keens the cast-out cat:
Miaow! Miaow! — a doleful din
And who will rise and let him in?

When slippery stones by the pond
Make filling a bucket an effort of will
And you're walled-up for weeks in the back of beyond
In a farm at the foot of a hell of a hill
Then it's early to bed, and thank heavens for that,
Till coldly keens the cast-out cat:
Miaow! Miaow! — a doleful din
And who will rise and let him in?

Fandango

No, I don't remember an inn,
Beloved.
I dimly recall a tent.
And the slow, sad sighs when I tripped on the guys
And the wondering what it all meant.
And the tears and the fears of the first time in years
That I'd been on my own with a bloke,
And the spreading and the tedding of the polyester bedding
And the tea that tasted of smoke.
And the reeds like swords
On the banks of the broads
And the bittern that didn't show
And the single-file walking that put paid to talking
And the pub
Where we didn't go.
The boozy halloos of the tyro crews
On holiday afloat
To the trudgingly
Begrudgingly
Decidedly curmudgeonly
Couple without a boat.
Never again
Beloved.
Never again
The looks of surpise in successions of eyes
As I told my traveller's tales
To folk who confided
That they'd thought,
As I did,
That we were going to Wales ...

To the Plasterers, to Make Much of Time

Scatter ye plaster PDQ
    Old Time is still a-flying
And this same gloop that spreads like glue
    In seconds will be drying.

That glorious lump of squishy stuff
    The tackier 'tis a-getting
The closer comes its "going-off" —
    (The nearer 'tis to setting)

That stroke is best that is the first,
    The more times ye do skim it
You take the job from worse to worst
    And push it past its limit.

Then be not slow, but boldly go
    And skim it now, or never
Or lumps will grow and bumps will show
    Which you'll regret forever.

A Letter to Gillian Clarke

Dear Gillian,

This is a bread-and-butter letter
Of the sort our mothers would have approved.

A letter of thank-you to the kind lady
Who took all her wisdom in a basket
And shared it happily with the poor.

A letter of admiration to the brave lady
Who turned herself easily inside-out
And let jagged people touch the soft side.

A letter of sorry to the bright lady
Who struck sparks from the company
And to whom I must have felt damp.

A letter of blessing to the silver lady
Whose music softened the edge of the wind's tongue,
Putting the sad gulls in parenthesis,
Filling the sea with oranges.

Manifold Manor   by Philip Gross   Faber £3.99

Who could resist verse so accessible?
A poet who can take us by the hand
And lead us, not into some alien land
But through what is familiar and possible
In words and metres we can understand.
"A book of verse about forsaken premises
And those who might have lived there", says the blurb:
And yet the book gives far more than it promises.
It may amuse, amaze, distract, disturb.
His verses offer facets of reality
Like little sequins. Here are grins and tears,
Humour and horror of encroaching years,
Odd intimations of mortality;
It's sad and stimulating, fierce and funny —
And worth four quid of anybody's money!

(The above appeared as a book review in the South Wales Argus)

Moortown in Oxford Street

In a posh West End bookshop, browsing politely,
Coming upon a poem about orf
And feeling, as it were, betrayed by it.

Standing on golden carpet, smelling pus,
Feeling the rough scabs, touching the helpless
Sealed-together Papageno-lips, and wondering
How many of the people browsing here
Knew orf. Knew sturdy. Even suspected
The thousand-and-one named scourges of a world
I'd folded up and left, thinking it safe
Till my eventual return to it.
Now here it was, and one of its sad facts
Held up for anyone to stare at it,
Take it at scar-face value from the book.

And then again,
Perhaps it was the poet I'd betrayed
By knowing he spoke only shepherd's truth.
Even a stark tale of the taking of life
Is hardly news to the one random reader
Whose fingers bear the purple lambing-stains,
Who knows the sharp smell of the wet birth-coat,
Has groped in crowded wombs for gristly feet.
Was all this simply a coincidence?

And in a corner of the shop, I wept.
Causing discomfiture among the staff,
Unsettling the other customers.
Snivelling for myself, and for the poetry —
Lying so long asleep in a closed book
Waiting a momentary congruence;
A single, sharp, exquisite relevance.

What Sophie Did

For Sophea Lerner

Sophie wrote a poem.
Thought it; drafted it.
Made, wrought, crafted it.
Brought it before a jury of her peers
And read it. Said it.

See all those words. Like ducks in a row.
Each one in its one-and-only place.
Sophie said so.

Then she decreed otherwise —
Upended their lineshelves.
Pulled out the wires through their middles
And spilled them. Killed them.

She took them and shook them
Because they had been stupid.
Hit them to teach them a lesson.

Then threaded them, chastened, all over again.
In a new pattern just as perfect
And equally flawed.

Hint to a child that there's no Father Christmas;
Prove to a poet there's no such thing as words!

Dumb on the jury, I applauded with the rest
Contributing to the consensus
Because there were no words left to trust.

I saw the poem and I closed my eyes.
I saw the poet,
Like a beloved child dancing on a high wall.
And I closed my eyes.

I dared not see; dared not say what I saw.
Youth itself. The power of it.
The daredevil juxtaposition of red and purple.
The calculated surprise of random numbers.
The insouciant creativity of the kaleidoscope.

One Hundred Words

(or a Welsh Incident)

Seeing a sickle beach, sipped by the sea,
Yr Wyddfa, sky-clad, shimmering above it;
Fistfuls of pebbles chattering to me.
Wishing I felt at liberty to love it.
But at my back I always seem to hear
The sound of matches rattling in the hands
Of xenophobic Welshmen, drawing near
To vindicate the spoiling of their lands.
If one should say "Your scenery's divine"
Would they feel complimented or supplanted?
Safest to claim their heritage as mine
And seem to take Snowdonia for granted.
No surer way to get it in the neck
Than spelling 'Cricieth' with a double 'c'!

To Piers Ploughman from Dick Ditcher

Standing astride a soft place. Thrust and thump,
Chopping a channel to take away water.
Threefold thrutching, cutting the clay all round.
Under and up they go, one after another,
Soft slabs a spade square, heaved onto the high side.
Look, the last lump, ultimate obstacle,
Gives with a grunt; a gurgling gush
Of waiting water rushes for release —
Tails to a trickle. Over. Ordinary.
Like last night's loving; leaves a little loss.
Another job jobbed. I unbend my back.
Damn all to do now. Leave it and go for lunch.

Stolen from Big Phyllida

An unsought insight into the greening of the Valleys

It was not mine. Big Phyllida said it
Right out loud in the Creative Writing Group.
"One thing I noticed, in the bath," she said
"The backs of my ankles don't get dirty now,
Not like they used to."

She who despises loudly what she calls "format"
She who says over and over that she "can't stand poetry"
She who claims to have read "only the one book"
(I never asked which, but my money's on *Das Kapital*)
Opened her silly, strident, soapbox mouth
And spoke poetry.

Out of her pursed lips it fell, like a small, new coin,
And neither she nor anyone, I dare swear, saw it fall.
Quick as a flash, I put my foot on it; changed the subject,
Went with the flow of tired conversation
And leftist cant.

But my mind crept down to where it lay unregarded
And I gathered it secretly safe into my hand.

I know I should have given it back to her —
"Here, Phyll — you dropped this" — knowing as I did
That this was the nearest she would ever come
To making poetry.

But if I gave it back, what would she do with it?
Nothing. She neither has nor desires the skill
To make a fit setting for it. She would only get it dirty
Like the grimy backs of her fat ankles
During the last desperate knockings of the Age of Coal.
She'd never miss it.

A familiar comfort. That's how I quieted my sullen conscience
When, as a child, I snaffled others' trifles
Which, I convinced myself, were unconsidered.
Their owners thus did not deserve to keep them;
This was not theft, more like a liberation;
I was the only one who knew how to love them
And they deserved me.

So it was with that special artless insight,
That delicious taste of the changed face of Wales,
That 'found haiku' that was almost lost
The day Big Phyllida let it drop heedlessly
When she opened her mouth in the Creative Writing Group
And spoke poetry.

River Girl II

For Wendy Cope — (who laughed)

Emmelina Butterbody-Brown was very large.
A girl of great complexity. She thought she was a barge.
This came to her quite suddenly one mild September day
As she trudged along the towpath in a dilatory way.
From Hammersmith to Putney she propelled her sixteen stone
Till she had a funny feeling she no longer was alone.
She peeped about her furtively till, right before her eyes
She spied a wild suburban boy, all speechless with surprise.
She lowered down her lashes then, the way the film-stars do.
And "pardon me, kind sir" she said, "for thus accosting you.
I was going to the pictures — but it's not much fun alone".
Then, blushing at her boldness, added "And I'm on the phone ..."

He was rude; he was ill-mannered — and he wasn't very nice.
He said "Garn — date all three of you? I can't afford the price!"
He added several epithets that sounded most unfit
Then made off in the direction of a blonde (peroxide) bit.

Emmelina Butterbody blubbered fit to burst,
Lamenting for her last love. It had also been her first.
She sank down on the towpath like a hippo at the zoo,
Her face besmirched with Kissing Pink and Periwinkle Blue,
Her hand upon her bosom in the region of the wound,
The sun a scarlet saucer over Fulham football ground,
Till, as the dusk was deepening from violet to black
A sudden something came about that brought her bouncing back.

Twixt her and Craven Cottage, all stately and serene,
There passed a giant timber barge that smelled of gasoline.

She gazed on this phenomenon until, before her eyes,
Out of the gloom materialised a buoy of wondrous size.
It was round and it was shining. It was sensuous and large
And it followed, sort of hopeful and resigned, behind the barge.

The barge gave not a hoot, but Emmelina gave a moan —
Here was a buoy whose size and whose devotion matched her own.
She gazed in silent empathy, then murmured tearfully
"Oh, leave your luckless loitering and come, oh come, to me!"

She rose and, under cover of the night, began to strip.
She gave a wave towards Barnes Bridge and whispered "Toodle-pip!"
She tiptoed to the riverbank and, with a whoop of joy,
She leapt into the water and struck out towards the buoy.

She touched his rusty pig-iron sides in one caress of bliss.
She touched his mooring mechanism with a languid kiss.
And then the waters of the Thames forever closed above her,
Embracing Emmelina and her monstrous metal lover.

"No Poems about Sheep"

For Daniel Baker, Wales 1990

Poets that are, were and would-like-to-be
Gathered around the wreckage of a meal.
A candle guttered, and the empties bred
In a damp cardboard box beside the door.
The veritas of vino grew in volume
As we contributed our several faggots
To the great fire that would purge Poetry
And set it free to soar to the great heights
That seem so accessible through damp glass.

O mes amis — pas devant les enfants!

Two eager eyes shone in an unlit corner —
Christ in the Temple, taking it all in.
The latest learning cohort, licking its lips,
Loving this revolutionary gospel.

Soon one by one we blundered to our beds,
Slept logly, and next morning saw our precepts
Framed by a child's hand, large upon the wall:
"No Poems about Sheep!" "No Birds of Pray!"
The acolyte had learned his lesson well;
We were weighed in his balance and found fun.

Later, I grieved. Poor child; what of his heritage?
Dragged rudely from the lap of Taliesin,
Taught to revile the secret, sacred signs
Of Welshness; raise two fingers to the Celt ...
Then I recalled how many Quests for Truth
Start with a smile. Poetry stood secure.
All we had challenged was its gravitas.
A muse is not disgruntled by a grin.
We took nothing away; we left him laughter —
A necessary weapon for a Daniel
At large among the literary lions.

For Later

When I am too old to enjoy obscurity
I shall become rich and buy a pub.
It will have sawdust, Real Ale and spitoons.
It will become a haven for True Artists.
Troubadours will assemble; poets converge —
I thought of calling it *The Harp and Party*.

THE SEVEN AGES OF THE SHE-POET

The Seven Ages of the She-Poet

1. CHRISTENING. The word-fairy offers the new-born poet her choice of the available voices of the aether.

The Christening is done. The tiny poet
Lies wordless at the centre of her world.
Godparents, who are feeling bored and show it,
File past the babe who sleeps with fists unfurled.

Over her cot the slippered fairy hovers,
Her flowered pinny twisted, toque awry,
Eager to wave her wand, bestow her favours,
Do justice to her buffet lunch, and fly.

Already she can see the trifle shrinking,
The *vols-au-vent* are disappearing fast.
(Typical, modern mercenary thinking,
Leaving the literary luck till last.)

The babe itself was nothing very special
And while she didn't mean to be unkind
She'd simply rattle off her special offers
And let the little sod make up its mind.

"What do you fancy, dearie? I am able
To grant you any voice you care to choose"
But she herself had one eye on the table
And two-thirds of the other on the booze.

"Auden and Eliot are standard choices,
Though for a girl they might be rather deep.
You could have either one of Wordsworth's voices —
I personally recommend the sheep.

Swinburne and Pope are both a tad pedantic
And Shelley nowadays a touch effete
But if you see yourself as a romantic
Then Lizzie Barrett might be up your street.

You might prefer Du Bellay's subtle *ton*, or
I do a lovely line in La Fontaine?
The streetwise cynicism of Villon, or
The deliquescent music of Verlaine?

You say the word; I'll do the necessary
Since it's no skin off my nose what you do.
There'll soon be nothing left to fill a fairy,
So make your little mind up PDQ!"

Sensing the angst, the baby howled and, hearing,
The fairy chose to take it as a choice —
An indication of the babe's preferring
An idiosyncratic tone of voice.

Her telescopic wand back in her pocket,
Her flowered pinny twisted, toque askew,
With all the grace and beauty of a rocket,
Fair for the food the famished fairy flew.

2. SHE WRITES HER FIRST POEM

Nothing remarkable. A lisp on paper.
Perfectly spelled; the scansion adequate
Provided you work out which words to lean on.

She keeps no record of the thing itself
But later may recall that it began
"Oh how I wish I had ...". A knocking bet;
She is a calculating little girl.

Later she will not call to mind the words
Much less the subject. But the praise, the praise!
The tilted heads, moist eyes and steepled hands,
The implication that she had "done well".
And the reward; the gentle revelation
That being read is being listened-to.

This is her first taste of the subtle joy
Of writing down something she dare not say
So as to pass it, like a folded note,
From a safe place behind a grown-up's chair.

Her mother has it still, though God knows where.

3. SHE WRITES HER 'TOAD' POEM

A found, or rather rediscovered, poem. Circa 1959 ...

The pool is still and the evening poised
Somewhere between violet and black.
We walk beside the water, throwing stones
And laughing. Why do you draw back?
What do you see? Why do you grimace without laughter?
I will go forward, you can follow after.
I will protect you. I am your guard and shield,
Alert for all your signals of alarm.
I will stand straight between you and your fear,
Protecting you from harm.
A toad crouches by the pool, stupid-blinking, and begins to crawl
With spastic haste from where we stand.
Your fear is now disgust. A toad. And was this all?
You shudder and I do not understand.
The creature reaches safety, and we wait.
The stupid gold-slit eyes peer from the warted face
And the humped back quivers with some reptile passion.
And then the horror is once more upon you, for the thing
Fixes you boldly and, assuming brute, attempts to sing.
A single note
Warped beyond bearing issues from the damp, pulsating throat
And I step forward, eager to remove
The cause of your distress and reaffirm my love.
I have brought you here to listen to me.
And the toad enters the water and is gone.
And yet that single, twisted note lives on
And even as I speak your name
The creature's ripples change, become a frame
And, as I watch, in them I see, twisted and quivering
An image of myself.

4. SHE WRITES HER 'DADDY' POEM

Long, long before she will come into her wisdom
She writes her necessary ode to Daddy.
Often a secret. Never a surprise.

Begun in spite
While stinging from some adolescent slight.
She word-weaves a wax Daddy and a world
To put him in. Stabs him in cross-stitch
On a lopsided canvas. Paints him in a landscape
Too quickly executed to convince
The connoisseur, and the whole thing
All set about with little implications
Of something sexually untoward.

And if she is at all unfortunate
Someone will publish it.
Then it will follow, grizzling at her heels
As once she did at his.
Rising at every public interview.
Up for Discussion. Never laid to rest.
Doomed to remain depressingly undead
(Unless impaled by a biographer)
Long after their progenitor has gone,
Slip-slid along the last path of most Daddies,
Dying by discernible degrees
In the unremitting custody of a good woman.

5. THE CRITICS TAKE NOTICE

Much of her stuff's a touch derivative
But none the worse for that. She makes you laugh,
Sliding the while an unsuspected knife
Under the third rib. You don't know it's there
Until you feel it grate against the bone —
A quick stab of familiarity:
Been there. Done that. Still wearing the T-shirt.

6. SHE IS SURPRISED BY INTIMATIONS OF MORTALITY

Long, long ago in the days of the Raj
My mother was brought up in India.
Once when the summer came to burn the plains
She went to Simla with my grandmother
And somehow her rag doll got left behind.
It was an ordinary little thing
By all accounts, but it had had two faces;
One smiled benignly while the other wept.
And Mother told me time and time again
Of how she ran to ask my grandmother
    "Mummy, Mummy! Where's my Dinah
    One face laughing, one face crying?"

I wished she hadn't told me about Dinah.
It gave me my first taste of impotence.
If I came to her with a tale of woe
She capped it with the story of that doll.
Childlike, I carried pain to her on trust
To have her soothe it with her sympathy
Not shame me with this awkward empathy.
It felt like hearing my father singing —
Uncomfortably inappropriate.
Mothers are not supposed to grieve for dolls,
Or stick pins in the conscience of a child
Who would but could not mend that old distress.

I grew to hate the maudlin little voice
In which she told the climax of the story —
    "Mummy, Mummy! Where's my Dinah
    One face laughing, one face crying?"

Some time ago, prowling an Oxfam shop,
I came upon a copy of that doll.
Someone had sewn it from a printed kit;
Probably a museum souvenir.
A flat rag doll. Decidedly two-faced;

One grinned inanely while the other wept.
I had to struggle with the urge to shout
    "Mother, mother — here's your Dinah
    One face laughing, one face crying!"

    So I bought the little bugger
    In response to inner prompting —
    "Loving gesture", "Sacred duty",
    But the voice that spoke the loudest
    Was the one that whispered archly
    "That's the last we'll hear of Dinah
    one face laughing, one face crying."

Next time I visited, I took the doll.
She thanked me, but seemed not to recognise
Just what it was that I was giving her.

After they took away most of the cancer
Mother came home and I moved in with her.
She was a small, decerebrated shadow;
I ill-at-ease with her new gentleness.
Once, on a bad night, helping her to bed
She stopped to rest and settled on her knees
Trapping her skirt so that she could not move.
Love made me clumsy and I stumbled, too.
We clutched each other and began to laugh.

    Giggling like a pair of schoolgirls
    Both precariously balanced
    Halfway up the narrow staircase.
    "Pull yourself together, woman;
    Less of this unseemly laughter!"
    "Hold on tight you silly bugger!" —
    Half concern and half affection —
    "Hold the banister, for God's sake
    Or we'll both be at the bottom!"
    "Hold me, mother — I'm your Dinah
    One face laughing, one face crying."

7. SHE WRITES HER OWN OBITUARY

One dark night in the middle of December
In the long thin hour between midnight and morning
Back came the fairy in a pinstriped costume
On her way home from a visit to her agent.
"Just called in to suggest an assignment —
What about thinking of a little opportunity
To put your own words in the mouth of posterity?"
Then she vanished, to return a bit later
Like the angel who visited Abou ben Adhem.
But the house was still and the poet was silent,
Slumped on her desk with her chin on her keyboard
In front of a screen that was covered with gibberish
Apart from a single, well-turned sentence —

"Spry she was, too, for such an old woman:
Could still turn a phrase like a chit of a girl."

FROM FURTHER AFIELD

Canal

A daft dream, pretending to be a river.
Mending God's oversight; He should have known
One should be here, this being Birmingham —
Going from here to there, look. Hubris or what?
Logical, but not on. Hardly a go.
But someone made it happen. Inch by inch,
All of a sudden, like a folly-pond.
Metal and wood, painted prostheses
Disguising Nature's disabilities.
God grinned and was not jealous, seeing the fun in it.
Ungainly, like sea-elephants. Good for a laugh.
A safe toy. Warm, well-meaning captive water
Smelling of farts from lock-bottoms. Silly. Implausible.
Black, white, brown-green and silver-grey
And standing for the power of gentleness.
Only an interrupted downhill progress
Singing along its length "See me; I can".

The Menhirs at St Pierre de Quiberon

After a long game of follow-my-leader,
Stumbling head-down, keeping out of range,
I saw my first 'alignments'. Granite chunks,
Lumpen, unlovely. Slummocked in a queue
Like students at a cashpoint on a campus.
Five almost-rows, but not quite half as straight
As teams of first-year infants at PE.
What Yorkshire folk call neither nowt nor summat.
A little grandeur, if you looked for it,
But mostly something awkwardly familiar.
I felt at home among the granite ghosts.

That odd one on the left — a little head
Balanced on tea-tray shoulders, carefully.
The weatherworn excrescence at its back
Suggested a small knapsack, carried high.
Its calculated military bearing
Seeming an effort to outpace the shadow
Of someone it would rather leave behind.
I knew that menhir. I had followed it,
Crestfallen, all the way from Quiberon.

And so it came as something of a shock
To lay a finger on its lichened surface
And not to feel it flinch.

The Ram's Skull

There it sits on the table.
An exercise in metaphor.
Eyeholes vacant;
Overstated horns akimbo.
Ridiculous in death.
The tutor speaks:
"Forget reality. See shapes. See thoughts.
See half-formed visions of a greater consciousness.
Just look and see and, having seen, say."

They look. I look. We look,
And one by one they speak,
Saying they see landscapes, caverns and waterfalls,
Great rocks and oceans and the homes of eagles.

Now comes my turn: "Ann, tell us what you see."
I see a ram's skull; heft it at arm's length,
Ponder in pantomime,
Then to the word-befuddled class declare
"Alas, poor Herdwick!" — and they roar
Till all that carefully constructed metaphor
Falls like a clown's trousers round the tutor's feet.

I feel myself dismissed — his tight lips telegraph:
"Trust you to settle for a cheap and easy laugh … "
Later, alone, I beg to contradict,
Such laughs are easy but they don't come cheap.

Who wants to be a poet anyway?
Sometimes I hate poets. Hate them for not knowing
The ram beneath the skull.

A Swaledale tup.
He'd have got bonny gimmers, this old chap —
For old he was; some of his teeth are gone.
See how the horns curl round and round again
Finishing in the comic little lift

Left over from his lambhood. Close and tight
They sat upon his cheeks, trapping his head
Till someone cut a slice from each of them
To ease the workings of his mighty jaw.
Somebody did a nifty hacksaw job;
Somebody else sweated to hold him still,
Digging their fingers into the greasy elf-locks,
Pinning his ear back with a grubby thumb.

Somebody cared. He'd not have lived so long
Without a good master. All of seven-shear.
Keen, too. See in one horn the drilled hole
Where they close-coupled him to a companion.
Ramshackled, lest they tupped the ewes too soon.

Seven times a fleece fell, damp and rank-smelling,
Stained with the old musk, bedewed on the skin side
With his essential oils. Oh, the rare stink of him
In the height of the season.

And once, on a latefrost morning, he was new.
Licked into life by an old blackfaced ewe.
Perhaps a child fed him and knew the touch
Of whiskery lips, the thrust of his blunt head.

How could they look at a ram's skull and not see
That once that skull would have been small enough
To fit roundly, slick as a cricket ball,
Into the cupped palm of a shepherd's hand.

"The longest journey begins with a single step ..."

A letter to Les Murray

I returned from a series of simple assertiveness sessions
And all I recalled as I dum-diddled home on the train
Was the answers I gave to a series of wearisome questions
In a bid to determine the dominant side of my brain.

I have tried very hard to release my creative potential
I have set aside time to improve my less tangible talents
I have struggled to contact the things I considered essential
And to summon my sensitive side to establish a balance.

But when I painstakingly put all the ticks in the boxes
And added the answers as I was instructed to do
I found myself thinking unbidden of dogs, fields and foxes
And certain that sanity lay in a letter to you.

What is more I am sure you won't tell me to look on the bright side —
Will appreciate how at the least it would leave me bereft
To discover that I, who so tried to develop my right side,
Appeared to be almost entirely devoid of a left.

But the shock has worn off and I'm facing the fact of my finding
And the world is still spinning and I am still up on my feet.
Being part of a tiny minority isn't worth minding,
Especially if you can think of it as an *élite*.

But I feel we could do with a special tattoo or notation
To help in determining which of the others is which;
It's a bind when you find that two-thirds of the whole population
Are living their lives on the opposite side of a ditch.

And although I don't know on which shoulder to carry the burden
Or which foot to lift when I'm taking that step to begin,
I accept that no matter how far I may wander from Eden
I'll be carrying with me a load of original Yin.

Across Wales with an Adjustable Hartington*

At Cricieth, in the station. Watching a race
Between an old man with a shopping trolley
And the approaching train.
Oh, brave old man!
Deaf to it; in defiance of it
He dot-and-carried his booty on bent wheels across the track.

The train stopped; the old fellow rattled on.
I and my briefcase and the Hartington
And our accumulated souvenirs,
A lot of pebbles and a few ideas
Slowly congealing into a masterplan.
Boarded the train. The southward trek began.

BARMOUTH

Barmouth. The doors open. Pandemonium
Spills its ill-favoured contents into the train.
Dear God, the smell of chips!
Lurid bermudas on unfortunate hips
Sucked-sticky stumps of rock mumbled by sulky lips.
They eat and eat, and the insistent beat
Of marching Walkmen leaks like old men's breath
From the illfitting plugs in grubby ears.
Their children whine a descant without tears.
And still they eat,
Their slack jaws masticating to the muffled beat
That stirs the air that smells of cheap-shod feet.

This is humanity at its least appealing.
For my soul's sake I imagine myself
A nun; a Little Sister of Compassion,
Moving along the aisles, smiling a benison.
Giving out texts and clean white cotton socks.

INTO THE ESTUARY

Things whizzing half-obscured by hedges of sea-holly;
Small boats skipping on an unquiet sea.
Brown ribbons of current tearing ahead of the tide
So as to beat it back to Bae Ceredigion.
I could jump now, into the singleminded eddies,
Bob like a bottle and be back in Cricieth soon, soon.

TYWYN

Here it was, on the outward journey, that we shed
The two old ladies.
From Shrewsbury they had conversed between sandwiches.
A knockabout of trivia, twanged back and forth
On over-strung voice-racquets. We listened with our eyes
Sliding now right, now left;
Passing with the advantage, slick as wet soap,
Across the invisible net in the cluttered aisle.
    "We have to change at *Mach* on this one, Mary"
    "It was to be expected, with his heart"
    "A bit of bicarb brings it up in no time"
    "Can I persuade you to an almond tart?"
Van in; van out.
Arguably one of the longest rallies in the whole history of verbal
                                                        tennis.

And it was at Tywyn that we lost them;
Arms like boiled bacon draping fat plastic bags
On one another until, bedizened,
They set off along the interminable platform.
The back of Mary's Crimplene dress
Was tucked in the waistband of her fleshcoloured knickers.
The further she went, the more her hefty thighs
Seemed to depend from a big, bare bottom.
The train stood still a long time at Tywyn.
Open-mouthed children watched her out of sight.

But now on the long platform there was no sign of them.
I realised that I had been hoping. Felt regret.
Felt and enjoyed a familiar discomfort.
Memory fishing for them like a dropped stitch.

ABERDYFI

Over the other side of the river
Something whistles to attract my attention.
Half blue, half green, scuttling silently,
Catching the sun from the mirror of the Dyfi.
A train. The train. Train from Aberystwyth
Racing with our train to beat it to the junction.
Single train. Single track. Singleminded purpose.
Must win. Must come first into Machynlleth.
Looks like a crayon, colouring the coastline
Pushed in the fist of a small, slow scholar
With his tongue in his teeth as he draws it towards me.
Three cheers for our train, first to Dyfi junction!
Yah Boo Sucks to the train from Aberystwyth!
Twice as long, half as fast! Four slow coaches.
Our train waits while it slinks into the station.
Sneaks in behind it, tosses it some passengers
And sets off back, arsy-versy, to Pwllheli.

MACHYNLLETH

A man in a check shirt, reading *I Bought a Mountain*;
Beside him on the seat
A rucksack with a map of Snowdon, obvious, once-used.

An aluminium draining-board, a gift from friends.

Painting the Kingfisher

I bought a box of watercolours
Just to paint round the kingfisher in my head
Once my 6B had trapped it on A5.

All of the old colours were there.
Sienna, a sunburnt plain where Garibaldi
And his draggled men marched in a ragged line.

Leaf Green. Limp-wristed. Like no leaf at all,
Lacking the quality of damp sunlight
That makes real leafness out of mere green.

Chrome Yellow, fierce and metallic
Piercing like fast cars coming out of darkness,
Looking like the taste of cheap sweets.

Lamp Black and Chinese White.
The leprous faces of old courtesans;
The soft smudge on the thumb that snuffs a wick.

Prussian Blue. Paradox. A pussycat
In boots; puff-chested paramilitary
Squiring Vermilion, the painted whore.

Square pans of colour. Surely the very bricks
To build a bird. Earthly materials
But not so far removed, surely, from God's.

There goes hubris; here slinks disappointment,
Like a sly lurcher at a poacher's heels.
My kingfisher was a caricature.

And back came the sick, hollow-bellied understanding
That first came on the day I realised
That the great stream of pictures that gave rise
To all that automatic praise — "That's nice — now do another one"
Were just a hamfisted kid's wet-weather scribbling.

In the sink, washing the brushes under the tap,
I watched kingfisher colours blur and coalesce.
Only the spurned yellow was still new in the box.

Tomorrow, on a new page,
I will try again. Sunflowers, possibly.
Or a yellow chair ...

The Ash Crook

When I first spotted the stick, it was spring;
To cut it would have made the old ash bleed.
Instead, I marked it with a bit of band.

All summer the stick wore an orange bow
To let the locals know that it was mine.
I claimed it in November; cut it off
Just where it forked in two — nibbled it round
First with my knife, so as to spare the bark.
Trimmed it to make a perfect, natural crook.
Left it to season on the granary floor.

I oiled and admired it. Turned it in my hand
Just for the pleasure of the feel of it.
It was a well-wrought thing; I cherished it.
One day I was careless and the old black sheep
Found it and naggled off great strips of bark
And ruined it. I mourned it for a day,
Then shrugged it off and made the best of it.
A working stick.
I sent the dog with it, caught lambs in the crook of it,
Leant into fierce winds on the strength of it.

It was one of the few things I brought away;
Not that it was costly or beautiful
But because I still like to walk with it
And feel the teethmarks of a good old friend.

CODA:

Air and Fruit

That's what he said he missed most, the Marquis*,
After they locked him up in the Bastille.
Contemporary documents reveal
That he was spared the rod.
They didn't even chain him to the wall.
He had a desk. Sat at it, truculent,
Writing complaints — *"Disgusted of Vincennes"*.
The food, he wrote, was of a quality
That bordered dangerously on obscene.
He railed at criminal cuisine. He whined
Not for the loss of lust and luxury
But for more basic things. Fresh Air. The liberty
To brush his lips against the sweet soft flesh
Of peaches. Smell the cider-sweat
On cool globes twisted from the yielding tree
And weigh the heavy pear upon his palm.
Ah, these he missed. Seductive nectarines;
Sharp-tipped asparagus; raspberry canes.
And cucumbers. Probably.

**de Sade. In a letter from the Bastille dated September 1784*